Read When...

To The One Writing The Letters....

If You Do Not Need Two Pages To Write Each Letter,
Please Feel Free To Create Your Own "Read When" Topics
On The Back Of Each Page And Add Them To The Table Of
Contents Page For The Wonderful Person That You Are
Writing This Book For.

To The Person Who Has Been Gifted This Book...

On The Following Pages, You Will Find A Table Of Contents
Where You Can Go To Quickly Look Up The Topic That
Applies To You At The Moment. Please Know That Each
Of These Pages Have Been Filled With Personal Heartfelt Messages.

Table Of Contents

Table Of Contents

Table Of Contents

Table Of Contents

Table Of Contents

Page Number	Question
_____	_____
_____	_____
_____	_____
_____	_____
_____	_____
_____	_____
_____	_____
_____	_____
_____	_____
_____	_____
_____	_____
_____	_____
_____	_____
_____	_____

You Receive This Book

_____

_____

_____

_____

_____

_____

_____

_____

_____

_____

_____

_____

_____

_____

_____

_____

_____

_____

You Can't Sleep

You Need A Laugh

You're Having A Bad Day

You Feel Like Giving Up

You Need To Know How Much I Love You

You want To Reminisce

You Feel Like You Aren't Good Enough

You Are Crying

You're Not Sure What To Do

You're Feeling overwhelmed

You Miss Me

You Need To Talk

_____

_____

_____

_____

_____

_____

_____

_____

_____

_____

_____

_____

_____

_____

_____

_____

_____

_____

_____

_____

You Are worried

It's Your Birthday

You Reached A Big Goal

You Are Bored

_____

_____

_____

_____

_____

_____

_____

_____

_____

_____

_____

_____

_____

_____

_____

_____

You're So Sad You Can't Talk

We Haven't Talked In Days

You want To Know Some Things
I Love About You

I've Just Left After Visiting With You

You Feel Insignificant or Insecure

You Need Prayer

whenever...

You want To Know one of My Favorite Memories of Us

You Need A Compliment

Before You Go To Sleep

You Need Encouragement

You Need To Know I Am Proud Of You

Life Is Hard

You Are Scared

You Are Feeling Sick

You Are Feeling Lonely

You Need To Make a Big Decision

You Don't Feel Appreciated

You've Done Something You're Not Proud of

You Are Procrastinating

You Need To Remember How Strong You Are

when You wake up

You Are Excited About Something

You Don't Feel Needed

You Are Disappointed

You Are Nervous

You Feel Distant

You Feel Left Out

You Are overthinking

You Are Having A Hard Time Forgiving Yourself For Something

You Are Angry

You Feel Like You've Failed

_____

_____

_____

_____

_____

_____

_____

_____

_____

_____

_____

_____

_____

_____

_____

_____

_____

You Feel Unattractive

You Need To Be Reminded That I Am Here For You

You Need Motivation To Keep Going

Made in the USA
Columbia, SC
04 March 2025

54671022R00061